St Antholin's Lecture 2020

PILGRIMS AND EXILES:
LEAVING THE CHURCH OF ENGLAND IN THE AGE OF THE *MAYFLOWER*

JOHN COFFEY

The Latimer Trust

Pilgrims and Exiles: Leaving the Church of England in the age of the *Mayflower* © John Coffey 2020. All rights reserved.
ISBN 978-1-906327-65-1
Cover photo: Mayflower II by Jim Curran on AdobeStock.
Published by the Latimer Trust August 2020.

This year is the 400th anniversary, the quatercentenary, of the sailing of the *Mayflower* across the Atlantic in 1620. The ship carried 102 emigrants, half of them English Separatists who had been living in exile in the Dutch Republic, in the city of Leiden. They were joined by 'Strangers', including skilled artisans recruited to help build the fledgling colony. Among the ship's passengers was the family of William Brewster, preaching elder of the separatist congregation. His two boys were named Wrestling and Love. For Brewster, the Christian life entailed both love (for God and neighbour) and wrestling — whether with angels or men. In the course of the voyage, one of the Pilgrims fell overboard and was hauled back on deck. One of the 'Strangers' died and was cast into the sea – according to one account he was 'a proud and very profane young man'. Despite this death, the ship arrived in the New World with the same number of passengers as when it set sail. A child had been born on the voyage and was named Oceanus.[1]

Unfortunately, due to two false starts, the *Mayflower's* journey had only begun properly in September, and as it crossed the ocean, autumn was turning into winter. After two months at sea, and blown far off course, the ship landed on Cape Cod in November. During the bitter months that followed, half of the settlers perished. The settlement only survived in 1621 because of assistance from the indigenous Wampanoag people, and from an English-speaking Native called Tisquantum (or Squanto), who had been kidnapped by English sailors in 1614, and had subsequently visited London, Spain, and Newfoundland. An alliance between the English and the Wampanoags was celebrated in a shared feast, the inspiration (from the late nineteenth century) for the American holiday of Thanksgiving.

The definitive contemporary history of the Plymouth colonists, which took the story from Scrooby via Leiden to America, was written by one of their number, William Bradford. He describes their joy on landing:

> 'Being thus arrived in a good harbour, and brought safe
> to land, they fell upon their knees and blessed the God of

---

[1] For a vivid account of the voyage see Nathaniel Philbrick, *Mayflower: A Story of Courage, Community, and War* (New York: Penguin, 2006).

Heaven, who had brought them over the vast and furious ocean, and delivered them from all the perils and miseries thereof, again to set their feet on the firm and stable earth, their proper element.'[2]

My own introduction to this historical episode came through a children's book. Around 1975, my mother took me on regular visits to a local bookstore to choose a Ladybird 'Adventure in History' book — I collected volumes on Julius Caesar, Alfred the Great, Christopher Columbus, Oliver Cromwell, and Napoleon, and by the age of six was already firmly set on the path to my future career — since I wasn't cut out to be a great military commander, I became an historian. (Those who cannot make history, can at least write it.) I remember being entranced by the pictures in the recently published Ladybird on the Pilgrim Fathers, especially depictions of Native Americans, firing arrows or feasting, portrayed inaccurately in the dress of Plains Indians from the American West.[3]

In the half century since that Ladybird book was published, our knowledge of colonial America and its Native peoples has been transformed. Thanks to remarkable research, brilliantly synthesised by David Silverman, we can now see the founding of New England from the Native point of view.[4] Against the inspirational tale of the *Mayflower* and its settlers, historians place the tragedy of Native New England, devastated by the Great Dying of 1616-19, when vast numbers of the indigenous population were killed by plague. When Tisquantum returned to his home village after his European sojourn (shortly before the landing of the *Mayflower*), he found it empty and desolate – wiped out by European disease. Here is a reminder of the dark side of European exploration and colonisation.

---

[2] William Bradford, *Of Plymouth Plantation* (New York: Random House, 1981), 69.

[3] L. Du Garde Peach, *The Pilgrim Fathers* (Loughborough: Wills and Hepworth, 1972).

[4] David Silverman, *This Land is Their Land: The Wampanoag Indians, Plymouth Colony and the Troubled History of Thanksgiving* (New York: Bloomsbury, 2020).

A year earlier, in 1619, another (unknown) ship had sailed into Virginia with a human cargo of twenty to thirty enslaved Africans. The *New York Times'* '1619 Project' has presented this moment — the landing of the first slave ship in the English colonies — as 'the country's true birth date, the moment that its defining contradictions first came into the world.'[5] This account of American history — in which America was built on the slave labour of Africans and the stolen land of Natives — has sparked fierce controversy and casts its shadow over the anniversaries of the *Mayflower* and the First Thanksgiving.

In this lecture, however, I will be focusing on England and the Dutch Republic, and on the decade before the *Mayflower*, a decade that witnessed some momentous religious developments that would leave their mark on future generations. The transatlantic migration of the Pilgrims was the result of another spiritual migration — before they left Europe, they had left the Church of England. Persecuted in the East Midlands, the Separatists had fled to the Protestant Netherlands for refuge, before sailing for America. In the reign of James I, this made them an oddity, but over the next two generations, hundreds of thousands of others would make this spiritual pilgrimage too. The seventeenth century began with a genuinely comprehensive national Church, with only tiny numbers of Protestant dissenters beyond it. It ended with an Act of Toleration that recognised the fragmentation of English Protestantism. Dissenters gathered in around two thousand different congregations — Presbyterian, Congregational, Baptist and Quaker — comprising over 5% of the English population. To understand the origins of this spiritual migration, we need to study pilgrims and exiles in the reign of James I.[6]

---

[5] pulitzercenter.org/sites/default/files/full_issue_of_the_1619_project.pdf.

[6] For overviews of the history of Puritanism and Dissent in the seventeenth century, see John Coffey and Paul Lim (eds.), *The Cambridge Companion to Puritanism* (Cambridge: Cambridge University Press, 2008), and John Coffey (ed.), *The Oxford History of Protestant Dissenting Traditions, vol. I: The Post-Reformation* (Oxford: Oxford University Press, 2020). For major single-author studies see Michael Winship, *Hot Protestants: A History of Puritanism in England and America* (New Haven: Yale University Press, 2018), and David D. Hall, *The Puritans: A Transatlantic History* (Princeton: Princeton University Press, 2019). An indispensable older work is Michael Watts, *The Dissenters:*

***

James, son of Mary Queen of Scots and veteran of the Calvinist Kirk, aroused the hopes of both Catholics and Puritans when he crossed the border to ascend the English throne in 1603. Both were to be disappointed. The Church James inherited was built on the Elizabethan Settlement — Cranmer's *Book of Common Prayer*, the Royal Supremacy, the *Thirty-nine Articles*. Elizabeth's Protestant regime had weathered the threat from Catholic Spain and the English people had acquired a firmly Protestant national identity. But the Elizabethan settlement was not without its ambiguities — it is a truism to say that it settled nothing, or nothing much — and there was a powerful lobby within Church and State for further reformation. From the 1560s, contemporaries began to talk of 'Puritans', hot Protestants within the Church. Some agitated for reform of the church's worship, while bolder spirits (the Presbyterians) called for an overhaul of its structures, and a few Separatists broke with the Church altogether, denouncing it as a false church, a second Babylon. The Presbyterian movement was stopped in its tracks in the 1580s, and a further wave of repression hit the Separatists in the 1590s — several of their leaders were executed for sedition.[7] Puritans channelled their energies into preaching and popular piety, developing a strain of 'practical divinity' that was promoted in hundreds of popular works, many translated into Dutch and German.[8]

In 1603, James found a Church that appeared to him far more orderly than the Scottish Kirk, where he had been troubled — and lectured — by aggressive Presbyterians. All but a tiny minority of the population worshipped within the parishes, and like his predecessor, he was determined to crack down on both Catholic recusants and Protestant separatists. In the Millenary Petition of 1603, Puritan leaders asked him to reform the ceremonies of the Church, and he met with them at the Hampton Court Conference of 1604, but although this would lead to the translation of the King James Bible, it was also followed by 141 new canons (or rules) tightening the requirements for clerical conformity,

---

From the Reformation to the French Revolution (Oxford: Oxford University Press, 1978).

[7] The definitive history is Patrick Collinson, *The Elizabethan Puritan Movement* (London, 1967).

[8] See Hall, *The Puritans*, chapter 4.

and prescribing strict subscription to the *Thirty-nine Articles*, royal supremacy, and the validity of the *Book of Common Prayer*. This prompted the largest ever purging of Puritans from the parish ministry — some 80 clergy were removed from their livings for refusal to conform. Yet very few Puritans were willing to follow their separatist brethren in giving up on the Church of England. By considering four aspects of the Church, we can understand why this was so.

First, in matters of doctrine the Church of England was clearly a Reformed Church. On the continent, Lutherans, Reformed, and Roman Catholic theologians agreed on this point. The *Thirty-nine Articles*, while less developed than the French or Belgic Confessions, was still recognisably a Reformed confession, more in line with Calvinists than Lutherans in doctrine.[9] When the Dutch Church was racked by disputes over Arminianism in the 1610s, James sent an English delegation to the Synod of Dort to endorse Reformed orthodoxy on the doctrines of predestination and perseverance. A few theologians did question Reformed teaching on predestination and perseverance, but generally these remained within the orbit of Augustinianism. An avant-garde was inclined to value the Fathers over the Reformers as theologians, but up until 1618 the centre of gravity lay with Reformed orthodoxy.[10]

Second, many Puritans had made their peace with the episcopal government of the Church of England. It helped that numerous bishops were staunch Calvinists in doctrine and Puritan-friendly in practice.[11] Richard Bancroft, archbishop of Canterbury until 1610, was a hardline conformist, but he was also firmly Reformed in theology. His successor, George Abbot — archbishop for the rest of James's reign — encouraged a strong alliance between conformist Calvinists and moderate Puritans. In the Church of Ireland, Archbishop Ussher was even friendlier towards Puritans, and his Irish Articles of 1615 were more emphatically Calvinist

---

[9] See Stephen Hampton, 'Confessional Identity', in Anthony Milton (ed.), *The Oxford History of Anglicanism, vol. I: Reformation and Identity, c. 1520-1660* (Oxford: Oxford University Press, 2017), chapter 11.
[10] See Jean-Louis Quantin, *The Church of England and Christian Antiquity: The Construction of a Confessional Identity in the Seventeenth Century* (Oxford, 2009).
[11] See Kenneth Fincham, *Prelate as Pastor: The Episcopate of James I* (Oxford: Clarendon Press, 1990).

than the *Thirty-nine Articles*, affirming the perseverance and assurance of the elect, and rejecting baptismal regeneration. Some apologists for the Church of England — including the erstwhile Puritan George Downame — were venturing *jure divino* accounts of episcopacy, and some wished to realign the Church by distancing it from Europe's Reformed churches. But England's leading divines mostly expressed kinship with the Reformed, and the Reformed in turn recognised episcopacy as a legitimate (if less than ideal) form of church government. In England, among early Stuart Puritans, there was no significant lobby for a Presbyterian reform of the Church.

Third, ceremonies presented more of a problem. Since the Vestiarian Controversy of the 1560s, many Puritan divines had objected to wearing the surplice, and they baulked at certain features of the *Book of Common Prayer* : the use of the sign of the cross in baptism and the ring in marriage, bowing at the name of Jesus, and kneeling at communion. The drive for conformity after 1604 landed many Puritan clergy in trouble with the law — as we shall see, some were briefly gaoled, and others went into exile in the Netherlands. Yet the enforcement of clerical conformity was patchy. While some bishops were zealous conformists, using visitations against the Puritan clergy, others turned a blind eye, valuing godly preaching above ceremonial conformity. And for nonconformists excluded from parish livings, there were ample opportunities to exercise one's ministry as a lecturer or the chaplain to a godly household.[12]

Finally, on the question of discipline, English Puritans looked longingly north of the border to the Scottish Kirk, where kirk sessions were proactive in disciplining ungodly members through rituals of repentance.[13] Yet while Separatists insisted that true churches must be purely composed of godly members, the great majority of Puritans took the Augustinian line that this was a Donatist error — the true church, in reality, was always a mixed company. The Lord's Table should be fenced,

---

[12] See Paul Seaver, *The Puritan Lectureships* (Stanford: Stanford University Press, 1970); J.T. Cliffe, *The Puritan Gentry: The Great Puritan Families of Early Stuart England* (London: Routledge, 1984).

[13] On discipline in the Church of Scotland see the magisterial history by Margo Todd, *The Culture of Protestantism in Early Modern Scotland* (New Haven: Yale University Press, 2002).

with the scandalous being barred, but the parish churches should comprehend the entire population. Puritans lamented the lack of effective discipline in their parishes, but they were also beginning to turn some towns and villages into models of godliness. Dorchester was a prime example.[14]

***

Thus while Puritans regarded the Church as 'half reformed' in its government, liturgy and discipline, for all but a few it was a true church. It bore the two hallmarks of a true church: the word was faithfully preached and the sacraments properly administered — even if it was somewhat lacking in what Anabaptists and some Reformed theologians (following Martin Bucer) took to be a third mark of the church, discipline.[15] To break from such a church would be to commit the sin of schism.

The clergy we call 'moderate Puritans' not only remained within the established Church, they also operated close to its heart.[16] William Perkins, the most distinguished practitioner of Puritan practical divinity around 1600, was also by far the best-known Church of England theologian in Europe. Lutherans and Calvinists were not reading Richard Hooker, whose writings remained in the vernacular, but they were reading Perkins. And Perkins was no nonconformist nor a Presbyterian — indeed, in the eyes of some scholars, he was so much a part of the establishment that it makes little sense to call him a Puritan.[17] He was, however, closely connected to the godly brotherhood centred on Cambridge, where Puritan clergy were ensconced within the colleges, above all Emmanuel College, the leading Puritan seminary, and the

---

[14] See David Underdown, *Fire from Heaven: Life in an English Town in the Seventeenth Century* (New Haven: Yale University Press, 1994).

[15] See Timothy Fulop, 'The Third Mark of the Church? Church Discipline in the Reformed and Anabaptist Traditions', *Journal of Religious History*, 19 (1995).

[16] See the classic study of Peter Lake, *Moderate Puritans and the Elizabethan Church* (Cambridge: Cambridge University Press, 1982).

[17] W. B. Patterson, *William Perkins and the Making of a Protestant England* (Oxford: Oxford University Press, 2014). See also J. I. Packer, *An Anglican to Remember: William Perkins, Puritan Popularizer* (St Antholin's Lecture, 1996).

source of many of the early New England ministry.[18] Its first master, Laurence Chaderton, had been present at the Hampton Court Conference, and he was frankly pragmatic about ceremonies: 'We may and ought to use them to purchase and procure liberty by preaching the Gospel'.[19] At Emmanuel, fellows had not worn the surplice in Elizabeth's reign, but Chaderton agreed to use it after 1604, while drawing the line at the sign of the cross in baptism. His successor, John Preston, enjoyed the patronage of the Duke of Buckingham, and was chaplain to Prince Charles. Such figures had strong connections to godly aristocrats and gentry. As conformable Puritans, they avoided conflict with the ecclesiastical authorities by making minimal concessions on ceremonial matters and admitting (if only grudgingly) the right of the magistrate to order 'things indifferent' (adiaphora) which were not determined by Scripture.

Yet there were others in the Puritan network who became marked as nonconformists. In some cases, this was due to the vagaries of enforcement. According to the 'Cheshire cat' theory of Puritanism, it could appear and disappear, depending on the observer. In Yorkshire, where the canons of 1604 were not enforced, the archbishop of York, Matthew Hutton took a tolerant approach towards nonconformity, valuing godly preachers who embraced the substance of Reformed religion. Elsewhere, respected clergy who fell under the jurisdiction of a diocesan itching to enforce conformity could suddenly be stigmatised as 'Puritans' or 'precisians.' Yet there was more to this than variation in episcopal policy. Some Puritans courted trouble because of a conscientious refusal to flex. They were less likely than their brethren to see the ceremonies as 'things indifferent.' Operating with a strong regulative principle, they challenged the authorities' right to impose rituals and requirements that went beyond the regulations of the New Testament. In the unreformed ceremonies of the Church they saw the remnants of popery: citing the Second Commandment, they called for the elimination of 'all the ceremonys & instruments of idolatry.'[20] Conformable Puritans regarded the most scrupulous nonconformists as

---

[18] For a magisterial study see Patrick Collinson, 'Puritan Emmanuel', in Sarah Bendall, Christopher Brooke and Patrick Collinson, eds, *A History of Emmanuel College, Cambridge* (Woodbridge: Boydell, 1999).
[19] Quoted in Hall, *The Puritans*, 184.
[20] Quoted in Hall, *The Puritans,* 173.

'weaker brethren', citing the Apostle Paul in Romans 14 on sensitive believers who refused to eat meat sacrificed to idols. Even if they were being overly precise, such weaker brethren should not be penalised. Yet many Puritans did suffer suspension or deprivation for their nonconformity.

A case in point is Arthur Hildersham, vicar of Ashby-de-la-Zouch, who was suspended and then deprived of his vicarage for refusing to subscribe to the Canons of 1604. His recent biographer notes his 'generally nonconfrontational approach to the authorities', but also describes how he fell afoul of the drive for conformity in the diocese of Lincoln.[21] After he was deprived, Hildersham was still able to preach in Derbyshire thanks to a preaching license from the bishop of Coventry and Lichfield, and he continued to enjoy support from the earl of Huntingdon, one of England's leading Puritan noblemen. In 1613, however, even his license to preach and catechise was rescinded by High Commission, and two years later, Hildersham was presented to the bishop for failing to receive communion kneeling along with nearly one hundred fellow parishioners. When he refused to swear the *ex officio* oath, he was imprisoned for three months, and then went into hiding in the home of one of his patrons. Hildersham continued to exercise significant local influence, and he was very well connected among the Puritan clergy and their patrons — yet none of this protected him from prosecution.

***

The pressure on nonconformist clergy led some to consider emigration. Exile had long been an option for dissenting clergy, from Henrician evangelicals and the Marian exiles to Elizabethan Presbyterians and Separatists.[22] By the early seventeenth century, the Dutch republic had emerged as the most attractive refuge, both because of its Reformed public church and its lenient policy towards religious outsiders — Catholics, Mennonites, and Jews all enjoyed a *de facto* toleration. In

---

[21] Lesley A. Rowe, *The Life and Times of Arthur Hildersham: Prince among Puritans* (Grand Rapids: Reformation Heritage Books, 2013), quotation at p. 88.
[22] John Coffey, 'Exile and Return in Anglo-American Puritanism', in Yosef Kaplan (ed.), *Early Modern Ethnic and Religious Communities in Exile* (Cambridge: Cambridge Scholars Press, 2017).

Amsterdam, John Paget became minister of the English Reformed Church, a congregation for expatriates that belonged to the Dutch Reformed Church and was thus presbyterian in its polity. As Polly Ha has shown, Paget and his congregation helped to keep English Presbyterianism alive during the difficult decades of the early Stuart era.[23]

In the 1610s, a number of eminent Puritan divines migrated to Leiden, including Robert Parker, Henry Jacob and William Ames (who became a professor of theology at the city's university). These figures articulated a congregationalist account of church polity, making the case for voluntary, self-governing local congregations formed by means of a mutual covenant between godly people. They forged a middle way, adopting elements of separatist polity while recognising that parish congregations could be true churches. Henry Jacob provided a succinct definition of the church: 'A true Visible & Ministeriall Church of Christ is a number of faithfull people joined by their willing consent in a spirituall outward society or body politike, ordinarily coming together into one place, instituted by Christ in his New Testament & having the power to exercise Ecclesiasticall government and all God's other spirituall ordinances (the meanes of salvation) in & for it selfe immediately from Christ.'[24] There was no need to tarry for the magistrate or for bishops — the godly could form their own churches independently of higher political or ecclesiastical authority.

Jacob put this theory into practice, returning to England in 1616 to establish a congregational church in Southwark, one that fellowshipped with both Separatist churches and Puritan parishes. This represented a major new option for the godly. It represented 'an irenic congregationalist third way between the separatists and the Church of England.'[25] Congregationalism would become the New England Way in

[23] Polly Ha, *English Presbyterianism, 1590-1640* (Stanford: Stanford University Press, 2010).
[24] Henry Jacob, *The True Beginning and Institution of Christ's True Visible or Ministeriall Church* (1610), cited in R. Tudur Jones (ed.), *Protestant Nonconformist Texts, vol. I: 1550-1700* (Farnham: Ashgate, 2007), 115.
[25] Michael Winship, *Godly Republicanism: Puritans, Pilgrims and A City on a Hill* (Cambridge, MA: Harvard University Press, 2012), 100. On Jacob's

the 1630s before surging across England in the 1640s and 1650s, protected by Oliver Cromwell and defended in print by John Owen.

The 1610s also witnessed important developments among the Separatists. Separatists took a very hard line against the Church of England, charging it with being a false church, a Babylonian limb of Antichrist corrupted by popish idolatry. Since the 1590s, Amsterdam had been the home of a Separatist congregation led by Francis Johnson. This 'Ancient Church' was roiled by internal troubles of its own, including sex scandals involving his associate, Daniel Studley, and a controversy over the fashionable dress of Thomasine Johnson, the pastor's wife.[26] Johnson shared leadership with Henry Ainsworth, one of England's most learned biblical commentators, who used his contacts with the city's Jews to improve his knowledge of rabbinic scholarship. But the two men eventually parted ways, with Johnson taking some members to Emden, and Ainsworth remaining with the rest in Amsterdam congregation. As so often in church history, separatists ended up separating from each other.

In 1608, other Separatists came to Amsterdam from the East Midlands, where they had been harried by the authorities. John Smyth had founded a Separatist church in Gainsborough, supported by a prosperous layman, Thomas Helwys. Meanwhile, John Robinson had formed a congregation at Scrooby in Nottinghamshire, meeting in the manor house of William Brewster, itself owned by the archbishop of York, for whom Brewster worked as postmaster. Once prosecuted for separatism, these dissenters could obtain no license to travel abroad. But by paying hefty fees to the captains of sailing vessels, they came — illegally — to the Netherlands.

Here, the two congregations diverged. Smyth took Separatism to its logical extreme.[27] Crucially, he came to doubt infant baptism. Different

intellectual originality and his disputes with more conservative Puritans see Polly Ha, ed., *The Puritans on Independence: The First Examination, Defence, and Second Examination* (Oxford: Oxford University Press, 2017).

[26] Martha Finch, '"Fashions of Worldly Dames": Separatist Discourses of Dress in Early Modern London, Amsterdam and Plymouth Colony', *Church History*, 74 (2005).

[27] See James Coggins, *John Smyth's Congregation: English Separatism, Mennonite Influence and the Elect Nation* (Waterloo ONT: Herald Press, 1993).

factors were at work here. Having repudiated the Church of England as a false church, and thus distanced himself from the Reformed churches, Smyth was ready to contemplate further breaches. (He would, for example, repudiate orthodox Reformed teaching on predestination; this was part of his realignment with the Anabaptists against the Calvinists, though it also aligned him with the Dutch Arminians.) In addition, Smyth like other Separatists was a radical primitivist, who sought to go back to the roots of the first-century apostolic church, before its post-apostolic declension. Lancelot Andrewes may have taught Anglicans to revere one canon, two testaments, three creeds, four councils, and five centuries, but for Smyth, *sola scriptura* entailed building one's theology on the Apostles alone, without reference to the Church Fathers. Because the New Testament did not explicitly teach that infants should be baptised, the practice was seen as a popish corruption. At the same time, Smyth accentuated the discontinuity between Old and New Testament, denying that the circumcision of infants in the old covenant supported the baptism of infants under the new. Infant baptism and national churches were hallmarks of a Judaising Christianity. Instead, Smyth intensified the Separatist belief that true churches were created by voluntary covenants between believers — since infants could neither believe nor make voluntary covenants, he reasoned, they could not be baptised into the church.

This logic led Smith to the doctrine of believers' baptism. First, he baptised himself, and then his followers. After doing so, he had doubts about the legitimacy of his self-baptism, and sought admission to the Waterlanders, a branch of the Dutch Anabaptist Mennonite sect. This in turn prompted a breach with Helwys who returned to England with a splinter group to found England's first Baptist church in Spitalfields. In 1612, Helwys published *The Mystery of Iniquity.* Here he condemned the Church of England as a second Antichrist, marked out as such by the practice of persecution. It may be no coincidence that this year also saw the execution of two anti-Trinitarians for heresy: one at Smithfield, the other at Lichfield.

Smyth was not to know that this was to be the *last* execution for heresy in English history, but later historians have seen his work as the *first* clear statement in English of a natural right to religious freedom. God alone, he argued, was Lord over conscience and 'men's religion to God is betwixt God and themselves.' Each individual was directly answerable to their Creator and should therefore enjoy 'freedome of religion' to 'chuse their religion themselves.' 'Let them be heretikes, Turcks, Jewes, or whatsoever, it appertains not to the earthly power to punish them in the least measure.'[28] He sent his treatise to James I with an accompanying manuscript note, which still survives: 'The King,' he said, 'is a mortal man, and not God, therefore he hath no power over the mortal soul of his subjects to make laws and ordinances for them and to set spiritual Lords over them.'

John Robinson was a less rigid Separatist than Helwys. 'For schism and division', said one of the Plymouth settlers, 'there was nothing in the world more hateful to him.'[29] When he moved with his congregation to Leiden, he formed a close friendship with William Ames, and a good relationship with the Dutch Reformed Church and the University of Leiden, where he taught against Arminianism. Although the Church of England, because of its popish ceremonies, was still 'Babylon', Robinson argued that Separatists could join with its members in private prayer, though not in its formal worship. Order and ordinances mattered, but they were not the heart and soul of 'religion and piety.' One had to distinguish between the idolatrous *parish assemblies* of England and their *godly members*, and between the corrupt 'order, ordinances and institutions' of the established Church and its doctrine: 'never church in the world,' wrote Robinson, 'in which so many excellent truths were taught, stood in such confusion both of persons and things, and under such a bondage spiritual, as that of England doth at this day.' Yet the Church of England had produced 'great fruit', many saints with 'personal graces', and 'divers martyrs', and it was recognised by 'the judgment of the other [Reformed] churches abroad.'[30] Robinson's most famous statement — that the Lord hath yet more light to break forth from his Word — was both an argument for further reformation and an expression of humility.

---

[28] Thomas Helwys, *A Short Declaration of the Mistery of Iniquity* (1612), 46, 69; Helwys, *Objections Answered by Way of a Dialogue* (1615), 30. See Robert Louis Wilken, *Liberty in the Things of God: The Christian Origins of Religious Freedom* (New Haven: Yale University Press, 2019), 181.
[29] Philbrick, *Mayflower*, 30.
[30] John Robinson, *Of Religious Communion, Public and Private* (1614), in Jones (ed.), *Protestant Nonconformist Texts, vol. I*, 118-24.

In Leiden, the Separatists enjoyed religious toleration, but they were discontented. They suffered economic hardship and cultural dislocation. They worried about their children going Dutch and feared a new war between Spain and the United Provinces. On top of this push factor, there was a pull factor: the tantalising appeal of the New World. The English colony of Virginia was beginning to find its feet after some harrowing times, and America held out the prospect of freedom of worship in an English colony three thousand miles away from the bishop of London, whose oversight of the colonists was merely nominal.

So it was that these exiled English Separatists began to plan for another migration. Not to seek religious freedom, something they already enjoyed, but to establish a godly English community across the ocean. Yet to make this dream a reality, they had to compromise, taking on board a motley crew of Strangers, with the practical skills to enable them to survive. And in America, they would have to negotiate (and eventually fight) with indigenous peoples whose religion seemed far more clearly idolatrous than the worship of the Church of England.

The story of the *Mayflower* has often been relayed as a heroic tale, and it has its heroic elements. It took genuine courage to transplant oneself and one's family across the Atlantic ocean and to set up a community in the American 'wilderness.' Yet like many later exiles from the Church of England, the Pilgrims discovered that the grass was not necessarily greener on the other side.[31]

***

It is worth emphasising, by way of conclusion, just how seminal was this single decade of English (and Dutch) church history. 1611 saw the publication of the Authorised Version, *the* Bible translation of Anglophone Protestant Christians for the next three-and-a-half centuries. The decade also witnessed the birth of the English Baptist movement and with it, the first explicit articulation in English of religious freedom as a principle that extended to all faiths, orthodox or heterodox, Christian or

---

[31] On the trials of the colony see John Turner, *They Knew they were Pilgrims: Plymouth Colony and the Contest for American Liberty* (New Haven: Yale University Press, 2020).

non-Christian. In the middle of the decade, Henry Jacob formed England's first congregational church, pioneering self-governing congregations that adopted an irenic posture towards the parishes. Here was an 'independent' ecclesiology with a bright future. In the Dutch Church, the Remonstrant controversy would mark the beginning of the long war of words between 'Calvinists' and 'Arminians.' Last, but not least, English Separatists founded Puritan New England, setting up America's first godly colony, Plymouth Plantation. Although preceded by Virginia and quickly overshadowed by Massachusetts, it would be Plymouth that captured the American imagination in the later nineteenth century. Both the voyage of the *Mayflower* in 1620 and the so-called 'First Thanksgiving' of 1621 would be incorporated into the creation myth of modern America.

Yet all this lay in the future. In 1620, it would have been easy to dismiss the Baptists, the Congregationalists, and the *Mayflower* Separatists. These were tiny groups, more visible in exile than in England. In a national population of around four million, only a few thousand met in dissenting Protestant congregations beyond the established church. While some left the Church of England by a formal separation, there were more who left it *de facto* by going into exile — but leaving the established Church was quite exceptional, even for Puritans. The vast majority of the godly remained deeply invested in the Church and would continue to fight for it until the Restoration, and (in the case of the Presbyterians) until the Glorious Revolution of 1688-89.

Remarkably, even the sects were led by men raised within the Church and trained in one of its seminaries, the University of Cambridge. Francis Johnson and John Smyth had been fellows of Christ's College; John Robinson a fellow of Corpus Christi; Henry Ainsworth had studied at St John's and Caius. But that posed a problem for the Church. The Separatist leaders were not unlearned plebeians; these fierce critics of the religious establishment came from within, from its educated elite. Charles I and Archbishop Laud would seek to tighten uniformity, and to clamp down on Puritan dissent. In doing so, they provoked a backlash that grew into a Puritan Revolution. In the long term, English Protestantism would be divided into Church and Dissent.

Previous St. Antholin Lectures

2011-2020

Andrew Cinnamond
: What Matters in Reforming the Church? Puritan Grievances under Elizabeth I

Peter Adam
: Gospel Trials in 1662: To Stay or to Go?

Lee Gatiss
: Edmund Grindal: The Preacher's Archbishop

Lee Gatiss
: "Strangely Warmed": Whitefield, Toplady, Simeon and Wesley's Arminian Campaigns

Richard Turnbull
: Transformed Heart, Transforming Church: The Countess of Huntingdon's Connexion

Martyn Cowan
: Portrait of a Prophet: Lessons from the Preaching of John Owen (1616-1683)

Kirsten Birkett
: And the Light Shineth in Darkness: Faith, Reason and Knowledge in the Reformation

Donald John MacLean
: "Ours is a True Church of God": William Perkins and the Reformed Doctrine of the Church

Matthew Rowley
: Toxic and Intoxicating: Puritan Theology and the Thirst for Power

John Coffey
: Pilgrims and Exiles: Leaving the Church of England in the Age of the *Mayflower*

Peter Adam	Word and Spirit: The Puritan-Quaker Debate
Wallace Benn	Usher on Bishops: A Reforming Ecclesiology
Peter Ackroyd	Strangers to Correction: Christian Discipline and the English Reformation
David Field	"Decalogue" God and his Seventeenth Century Bestsellers: A 400th Anniversary Appreciation
Chad B Van Dixhoorn	A Puritan Theology of Preaching
Peter Adam	'To Bring Men to Heaven by Preaching': John Donne's Evangelistic Sermons
Tony Baker	1807-2007 John Newton and the Twenty-First Century
Lee Gatiss	From Life's First Cry: John Owen on Infant Baptism and Infant Salvation
Andrew Atherstone	Evangelical Mission and Anglican Church Order: Charles Simeon Reconsidered
David Holloway	Re-establishing the Christian Faith - and the Public Theology Deficit

Lectures from 2001-2010 are compiled in *Preachers, Pastors, and Ambassadors: Puritan Wisdom for Today's Church.* Edited by Lee Gatiss.

1991-2000

J.I. Packer	A Man For All Ministries: Richard Baxter 1615-1691
Geoffrey Cox	The Rediscovery and Renewal of the Local Church: The Puritan Vision
Alister E McGrath	Evangelical Spirituality: Past Glories, Present Hopes, Future Possibilities
Gavin J McGrath	'But We Preach Christ Crucified:' The Cross of Christ in the pastoral theology of John Owen 1616-1683
Peter Jensen	Using the Shield of Faith: Puritan Attitudes to Combat Satan
J.I. Packer	An Anglican to Remember - William Perkins: Puritan Dilemma
Bruce Winter	Pilgrim's Progress and Contemporary Evangelical Piety
Peter Adam	A Church 'Halfly Reformed': The Puritan Dilemma
J.I. Packer	The Pilgrims' Principles: John Bunyan Revisited
Ashley Null	Conversion to Communion: Thomas Cranmer on a Favourite Puritan Theme

Lectures from 1991-2000 are compiled in *Pilgrims, Warriors, and Servants: Puritan Wisdom for Today's Church.* Edited by Lee Gatiss.

Other St Antholin Lectures

Toxic and Intoxicating. Puritan Theology and the Thirst for Power by Matthew Rowley

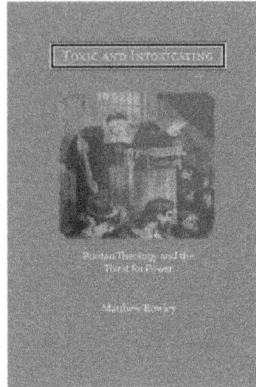

The thirst for power changed Puritan theology, often in ways that went unnoticed. The rise and decline of political puritanism afforded unique theological temptations. As victors or victims, many approached cultural conflict with a deep sense their cause was righteous — and this often blinded them to the ways they victimised others. This lecture focuses on the darker moments of Puritan history and explains how some of their worst actions flowed from good intentions and admirable qualities. I explore nine ways their theology staggered under the influence of politics. We must remember this history and learn from it if we are to avoid toxic and intoxicating mixtures of piety and patriotism!

Ours is a True Church of God. William Perkins and the Reformed doctrine of the Church by Donald McLean

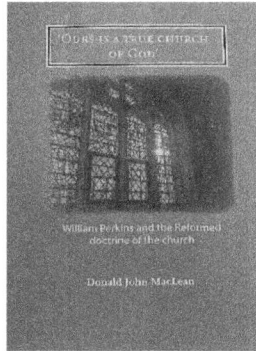

How do we discern a "true" church? Given the current ecclesiastical climate this is an increasingly pressing question. This study looks at how William Perkins, a great seventeenth century Church of England theologian, responded to this issue.

Particular focus is given to his understanding of the distinctions between the visible and invisible church, and the marks of a "true" church, namely, word, sacraments and discipline. Judged against these marks, Perkins argued passionately that the Church of England was "a true church of God".

He also, in line with traditional Reformed ecclesiology, allowed significant doctrinal and practical decline before a church ceased to be a "true" church. The criteria he outlined for leaving a church amounted to nothing less than the obstinate and persistent overthrow of cardinal Christian doctrine and worship.

Perkins' careful teaching calls us to consider our response to declension in the church today. Ultimately his ecclesiology calls us to have a high view of the unity of the visible church, and in many causes to labour for recovery rather than to leave.

And the Light Shineth in Darkness. Faith Reason and Knowledge in the Reformation by Kirsten Birkett

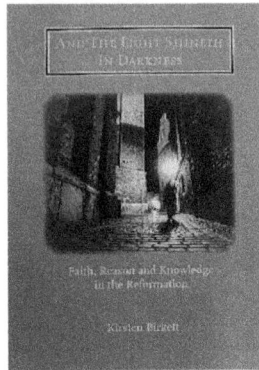

The Bible describes a fallen world and fallen humanity, in which minds are darkened. We reject God and suppress the truth about him. How, then, can we know him at all? In other words, what are the noetic effects of sin? During the Reformation, doctrines of total depravity and the effects of the fall on the whole person re-emerged, with consequent implications for epistemology. If minds are fallen, how can we expect to know anything accurately? The purpose of this study is to start to answer that question by looking at some of the epistemology we find emerging from the writings of John Calvin and Martin Luther.

www.ingramcontent.com/pod-product-compliance
Lightning Source LLC
Chambersburg PA
CBHW030013040426
42337CB00012BA/771